MW00872548

HOW TO SURVIVE IN NEW YORK CITY

AS TOLD BY ONE OF THE NYPD'S

TOP ANTI-CRIME DETECTIVES

BY MIKE GREENE

SECTIONS:

ABOUT MIKE

I started my law enforcement career at age 16, when I became an Auxiliary Police Officer for the New York City Police Department. The minimum age to join was 17, but my recruiter snuck me in to meet his recruitment goals. I worked in the 19th precinct, in the borough of Manhattan. Most of my friends said I was a fool. The position required me to wear a police uniform and patrol assigned areas at least 4 hours per week, without a salary and without a gun. This was a time when New York City was the most dangerous and crime ridden city in the nation. I was a bold city kid and didn't know any better. During the next three years, I made a few felony arrests for pickpocketing, assault and armed carjacking and performed crowd control and medical emergency duty.

At age 19, I joined the United States Postal Inspection Service, Narcotics Division, as a Confidential Investigator. The USPS is arguably the oldest federal law enforcement agency, dating back to the days of The Pony Express. I was tasked with assuming fictitious identities and working within and outside of Post Office facilities in an undercover capacity. I befriended Postal and non-Postal Service employees who were selling crack and heroine to Postal employees. While wearing hidden electronic recording devices, I would purchase crack and heroine from these drug dealers. Over a two year period, I found myself in the then burnt out and abandoned crack houses of the South Bronx and in the crime filled streets of Hell's Kitchen, Manhattan. I had guns pointed against my head and fought for my life on a handful of occasions. For a salary of $7 per hour, this job was extremely dangerous and not worth my life. I resigned after two years of service.

Two months after my 22nd birthday, and two years after taking the entry level written examination and passing background checks, I joined the NYPD. My Police Academy class was the largest in NYPD history, with approximately 3,000 recruits, and reporting for duty on my first day of training at midnight. It was June 30th, 1992, 3,000 of us, wearing suits and ties, packed into an high school auditorium built to built to hold a few hundred. Ambulance crews were on scene as many recruits passed out from heat exhaustion in the 90 degree heat in the auditorium . This was a sign of future things to come. At the Police Academy, the gym locker rooms were built to handle one hundred recruits, but each of our gym classes consisted of a few hundred recruits. We had three hundred men of varying sizes squeezed into a locker room built for one hundred. We had an open shower room with 10 shower heads and drains that were always clogged as you bathed in dirty standing water, in 90 degree heat and without air conditioning. We sucked it up and dealt with it for six months.

In January, 1993, my first post Academy assignment was Midtown North Precinct. Some of the neighborhoods in this area included Hell's Kitchen and Times Square. Looking back at the crime statistics that year, I realized that I was working in a truly crime ridden environment. In 1993, in NYC, there were 1,927 reported murders, 3,225 reported rapes, 85,892 reported robberies, 100,936 reported burglaries, 85,737 reported grand thefts and 111,622 reported car thefts. Compare these 1993 stats to the 2012 stats (when I retired) of 417 reported murders, 1,445 rapes, 20,144 robberies, 19,170 burglaries, 42,721 grand thefts and

8,053 car thefts. My 20 year career would have me right in the heart of the most historic reduction in crime by any police department on the planet. *Compare these stats to the entire state of Florida. In 1993 there were 1,187 murders and in 2012 1,009 murders. These are stats I've saved to memory for some time.

I quickly realized what I knew prior to joining the NYPD, I loved the job. During most of my career, I had supervisors that gave me an extreme amount of freedom. Most of the time I was unsupervised. This freedom allowed me to use my think outside of the box creativity, ambition and drive to develop and implement my own crime reduction strategies. I was a uniformed beat cop, working the streets of gritty Midtown Manhattan. My shifts were 5:30pm to 2am and 7:00am to 3:30pm. Community policing was not taught to me, it was a natural part of my personality and character. I would walk the beat and speak with every shop owner on my post. We would not only discuss crime issues, but everyday life and their personal issues. This was genuine, but also helped improve community and police relations. We were both stakeholders in keeping the area safe. I developed non -

traditional methods to observe criminals while they committed crimes, then apprehended them. I was able to reduce crime on my posts by 100%, completely eliminating crime on my posts.

In 1994, I was assigned to the precinct's Summons Unit. My shift was 7am to 3:30pm. My goal was to issue 20 moving violation summonses per day. I was assigned to a marked or unmarked police vehicle and I had free reign of the entire geographical boundaries of the precinct. I loved the freedom. I was a crime fighter though, not a ticket writer. I used this freedom to roam the precinct and search for criminal activity. Other members of this unit rode in three wheeled scooters and sought to write an allocated number of parking tickets then would go home. I had a heart though and understood that these tickets cost money and would hurt the average working man or woman. I opted for only issuing citations for equipment violations such as broken tail lights. If the motorist fixed the problem within 48 hours, then the ticket would be dismissed and there would be no fine. I would then focus my day on catching criminals.

In 1995, I received a temporary assignment to the Manhattan Fugitive Apprehension Team. Our office was based in the Bronx, alongside of the Bronx Fugitive Apprehension Team. We were a plainclothes unit, responsible for locating and apprehending fugitives wanted in NYC. We had two shifts, 4am to 12 noon and 2pm to 10 pm. As typical with each of my assignments, most shifts lasted well beyond their 8 hour time frame. I traveled throughout New York City, New York State and other states, tracking and apprehending fugitives. I was tasked by my commander to increase fugitive apprehensions. Thankfully, once again, I was given freedom to do my job and roam the city, state and other states unsupervised. I created and implemented a very innovative strategy that increased fugitive apprehensions by 800%.

Shortly after completion of this assignment, I received a temporary assignment to the Street Crime Unit. We worked from 6pm to 2am and were based out of a secret facility on a small island located between Manhattan and Queens, Randall's Island. We were a small plainclothes unit tasked with taking illegal guns off the street. Our focus was shooters, armed burglars, armed rapists, armed robbers and other criminals who possessed or used guns or machine guns to commit crimes. This unit was something directly out of an action packed cop movie. We were engaged in shootings and/or gun related foot and vehicular pursuits multiple times each night. Our then Chief of Department indoctrinated us into the unit with the equivalent of a pep rally in a room where we all sat in a circle, chanting, "We own the night!" We were taught to not fear and to believe that we did own the night and that we were invincible. We did think we were invincible. I recall two specific vehicular pursuits with armed perpetrators where my team members and I did not have our guns. We were invincible, hardcore crime fighters, so we continued each pursuit. By the grace of God, in each of these situations we were not shot.

After my temporary stint in the Street Crime Unit, I spent the next five years in the Midtown North Precinct Anti-Crime Unit. I worked the 6pm to 2am shift and the 10am to 6pm shift. It was a plainclothes unit and we were responsible for patrolling on foot or in unmarked vehicles. Again, with a tremendous amount of freedom, I was allowed to create, develop and implement my own crime fighting strategies. I studied and learned peoples behavioral patterns. On a daily basis, I would scan crowds of tens of thousands of people and search for those people who's behavioral patterns and actions didn't fit. I would then spend hours following them, undetected, throughout the city streets. I'd observe them as they prepared to commit crimes, while they committed crimes and after they fled from their crime scenes. I was able to become an expert at predicting if, when, what type and how a person would commit a crime. In total, I was able to witness approximately 1,000 crimes. These criminal acts included armed robbery, grand theft, pickpocketing, burglary, sex crimes, car theft, car break ins, credit card fraud, etc. During this period, I served as the Team Leader of my unit, showing my colleagues and supervisors how to detect these criminals before they committed crimes and how to have a 100% conviction rate. I developed and implemented innovative collaborative public and private security strategies that decreased targeted crimes from 50% to 100% (completely eliminating certain targeted crimes).

My next assignment was the Midtown North Detective Squad. We were the guys in suits and ties who would arrive at the crime scene after the incident occurred. We investigated every crime that required further investigation and was not completed by patrol officers. These crimes included, murder, rape, robbery, credit card fraud, identity theft, domestic violence, terrorism, contract fraud, embezzlement, bank robbery, wire fraud, extortion, etc. Because of the area we were in, many of our cases were high profile. Trump, Saks 5th Avenue, St Patricks Cathedral, Consulates, the NYC Passenger Ship Terminal, Fox, CNN, NBC and CBS studios were located within the precincts geographical boundaries. This was the unit that destroyed marriages. Our typical work week lasted 80 hours, sometimes more and other times less. Every precinct had a dormitory room, full of bunk beds. Those dorm rooms were used every night. I'd go to work at 4pm on a Monday and fully expect to not return home until sometime on Tuesday or Wednesday. I caught up to 300 cases per year and assisted with another 500 or so cases per year. My claim to fame in the office was my ability to detect and determine when people were lying. I was dubbed "the human lie detector". Amongst the hundreds of arrests I made in this unit, some of my proudest were false report arrests. One of my last false report cases involved a woman who had scratch marks on her face and reported that she was raped outside of St Patrick's Cathedral. Everyone from the Precinct Commander to the ambulance and hospital rape counselors believed her story. Why not? She was in tears and had scratch marks on her face and arms. Before the international media was notified, I was sent to speak to her. It took me 10 minutes to realize that she had lied. It took me two weeks to determine that she sustained her injuries after a physical altercation with her boyfriend. She reported the rape because she did not want her boyfriend to get into trouble and she had to explain how she was injured. Some of my other notable investigations included the 9/11/01 World Trade Center terrorist attack, the 2001 NBC Studio anthrax attack, the 2010 Times Square car bomb terrorist attack, the US Airways plane crash into the Hudson River, foreign espionage cases, a national level identity theft case, an international kidnapping case, the Times Square Military Recruiting Station bombing, the British and Mexican Consulate bombings, etc. While in this unit I also served as a first responder, rescuer and survivor of the 9/11/01 World Trade Center terrorist attack. I served as a first responder, investigator and quarantine officer (myself quarantined as well) at the 2001 NBC Studio anthrax terrorist attack. I served as a first responder, rescuer and investigator of the US Airways plane crash into the Hudson River.

Collaterally, I also joined the Hostage Negotiation Team. The NYPD Hostage Team was the first police hostage team in the United States. The majority of the hostage incidents involved emotionally disturbed persons who were trying to kill or harm themselves and/or others. I also served in the Dignitary Protection Team. I was called upon a few times per year to work with foreign, federal and state protection agents, protecting foreign and U.S. heads of state. These protectees included the Prime Minister of Israel, the President of Israel, the Prime Minister of Canada, the FBI Director, the Speaker of the House, the President of the Dominican Republic and others.

I retired from the NYPD on June 30th, 2012, exactly 20 years from the day I joined. I loved my career with the NYPD, but it was time for me to go. Freedom to love your job and create innovative ways to be successful at your job became frowned upon as new leaders commanded the Department. Each leader wanted to make their permanent mark on the Department. This quickly developed into micromanagement. I was not one to be micromanaged. My spirit would not allow it. Fighting crime and protecting others though is still my love and passion. This is why I have written this book. I hope that after you read this book you walk away with new information that will allow you to visit New York City without becoming a crime victim.

I would like to say thank you to my Mother for supporting me throughout all of my law enforcement endeavors. I would also like to acknowledge and praise three men in the NYPD who helped me become a successful crime fighter. These men are Sergeant Ronald Brooks, the late Deputy Commissioner Jack Maples and Police Commissioner Bill Bratton. These men are true innovators who I have learned volumes from. Thank you.
                    - MIKE GREENE -

THE BOOK

I decided to write this book because of my love for helping others. I served a good portion of my career working in the high crime tourist areas of New York City. I watched, witnessed and investigated tens of thousands of crimes. Most of those crimes had one thing in common, they were preventable. I'm not giving the criminals who committed those acts a pass. We should be able to go into a restaurant, leave our bags on the table, walk away and return five minutes later and have our bags still there. That way of thinking though will make you a victim. Life is not all unicorns and rainbows. There are some that walk amongst us and see us as their prey. Some of these perps (perpetrators) are opportunists, while others are full time criminals, committing eight or more hours per day to conducting criminal acts. I want to empower people and help put these criminals out of business.

I wanted to write a book that was easy to read and not a novel. I want you to be able to read the entire book within an hour and walk away with a general grasp of how to be safe while in New York City. I also want you to read the book and know that what you are reading is genuinely coming from me, a veteran NYPD Detective, and not a professional author. I have not hired any editors or proof readers to filter through this book. I want you to read this book and feel as though I'm actually talking to you face to face. I want you to know that you're getting the real deal, straight from the horse's mouth and from the front lines.

When you finish reading this book, I want you to have a solid understanding of the number one way to protect yourself, awareness. I want you to understand that YOU are ultimately responsible for your own safety, not the police. I want you to understand that most crime could be prevented if victims had simply been more aware of their surroundings, followed their instincts and took responsibility for safeguarding their own property. I promise you that you will walk away from this book with life lessons that will keep you safe not only in New York City but in any city in the world.

Crime and criminals have no boundaries.

Stay safe my friends.

- Mike Greene -

YOUR ARRIVAL

Airports.

There are several airports in the New York City region. The three major airports are Newark/Liberty International, John F. Kennedy International (J.F.K.) and La Guardia. If you are traveling to New York City by air, chances are high that you will be arriving at one of these airports.

Newark/Liberty International is located in Newark, New Jersey. JFK and La Guardia are located in New York City (Queens). The primary police agency serving these three airports is the Port Authority Police Department of New York and New Jersey (PAPD). PAPD officers have full police authority in the states of New York and New Jersey, although their primary areas of authority are various international and interstate airports, bus terminals, tunnels and waterfronts in NY and NJ.

Your biggest concern while in the airport should be your luggage. Luggage theft usually occurs in dining areas, the luggage carousel areas, curbside or at the screening areas. These thieves are looking for unattended luggage and your inattentiveness. In simple terms, they are looking to see if you have left your luggage alone or are not paying attention to your luggage. The simple solution to this problem is to always keep an eye on your luggage and/or keep them in your possession. These thieves do not want to confront you. They are looking to do their deeds without confrontation.

Train Stations.

There are numerous passenger and freight railroads that operate in New York City. I will focus on the two interstate passenger railroad terminals, Pennsylvania Station (Penn Station) and Grand Central Station. They are the two busiest rail stations in the nation. Penn Station connects New York City with the rest of the United States, while Grand Central Station connects New York City with the suburbs of New York City and Connecticut.

There are two primary police agencies in Penn Station. These two agencies are Amtrak Police and MTA Police. Amtrak Police are actually private corporation police officers and do not work for any government agency. They garner their power and authority from private railroad police laws that date back to the 1800's. MTA police officers are government police officers with statewide police authority. The MTA Police Department was recently formed after a merger between the Long Island Railroad Police and the Metro North Railroad Police.

By definition, train stations consist of transient populations. When passing through Penn Station you will encounter throngs of people traveling to one of the many municipalities on Long Island, north to cities like Boston, south to cities including Washington, D.C. and elsewhere in the United States. Some are also daily commuters heading home or to work for the day. Mixed in with these crowds of people on a mission are another group of people who are in the station for other reasons. These people include the homeless, EDP's (emotionally disturbed people), drunkards and criminals. This means that you may encounter people who are talking to themselves, asking for money, visibly unkept, etc. Don't be alarmed. Just continue on your way.

Grand Central Station is patrolled by MTA Police. Unlike Penn Station, there are a noticeably lower number of vagrants in Grand Central. The general feel of Grand Central is safer and cleaner than Penn Station.

The majority of criminals, at both stations, are looking to steal your property. Similar to the airports, the majority of these criminals are looking to steal your unattended property. If you set your bags down and walk away from them or stop paying attention to them, expect the chance of your bags being stolen to increase. Once again, the simple solution to this crime problem is to keep and eye on your bags or hold your bags at all times.

Bus Terminals.

There are two main passenger bus terminals in New York City. One is located on 8th avenue and 42nd street and the other is located at the foot of the George Washington Bridge. Both are located in Manhattan. The 42nd st. terminal is the largest and busiest bus terminal in the nation. The primary police agency for the terminals are the PAPD.

The vagrant and criminal elements in the bus terminals are much more visible than at the airports and train stations. You'll need to be wary of the same crimes and issues that I've warned you about in the airports and rail stations, however there are other criminal elements present in the bus terminals. Inside and outside of the bus terminals, you will find pimps, pickpockets, sex offenders and other assorted perps (perpetrators). The pimps are there to prey on the underage runaways that arrive at the terminals daily. The other perps are not necessarily there to commit crimes, but they are present because a New York State Parole Board office is located around the corner from the bus terminal. These are convicted criminals, many with no or low paying jobs. More so than at the airports and train stations, I advise you to be very alert and aware of your surroundings while in or around the bus terminals.

Cruise Ship Terminals.

There are two Passenger cruise ship terminals in New York City. They are the Red Hook, Brooklyn terminals and the Midtown Manhattan terminals. There are four police agencies that have jurisdiction at these terminals. These agencies are the NYPD, the PAPD, the WCNYH Police (Waterfront Commission of New York Harbor) and the U.S. Department of Homeland Security (DHS). There are also private security companies that patrol these areas daily.

The terminals themselves are fairly safe. Very rarely do crimes occur on the piers. Most of the criminal activity in these areas occurs onboard the ships. These cruise ships can hold thousands of people. They are mini floating cities. As with any city, there will be crime. I've conducted missing person, sexual assault, domestic violence, assault, robbery, grand theft and other investigations aboard these vessels. The best way to protect yourself while aboard these ships is to remember that you are on vacation, but you are still living and playing around strangers. You do not know the criminal or emotional backgrounds of your fellow passengers. Just because you are on vacation does not mean you should throw away all of your common senses. Have fun, but still be aware of your surroundings.

You should also be aware of a few little known facts about cruising. The Captain of the ship can throw you off at any port and you are not entitled to any refund, etc. If a crime happens in international waters, the FBI investigates the incident. If a crime occurs within the nautical boundaries of another nation, that nations police force(s) investigate. If the crime occurs within New York Harbor, the NYPD, PAPD, DHS or WCNYH can or may investigate. Generally, the FBI will take the lead on most investigations and present these cases to the U.S. Attorneys Office for prosecution. Generally, the U.S. Attorney's Office will not prosecute crimes they deem to be low level. I have seen their office decline to prosecute serious violent felony crimes. I've had perps stand in front of me and confess to committing crimes. I've had badly injured crime victims in front of me and I've had to release the perps and explain to the victims that there was nothing we could do.

Anecdotes.

I was at the office and received a call from a
patrol officer who was at the Midtown
Manhattan Passenger Cruise Ship Terminal.
He said he had a situation and wasn't sure
how to handle it. I responded and boarded
the docked cruise ship. I took an elevator up
to one of the upper decks, where I met with
the Captain, Head Security Officer and a
man who was being held in the ship's jail
cell. The man confessed to beating a fellow
passenger the night before. I then spoke
with the victim. He was a 15 year old boy
and was with his parents. His entire face
was bruised, swollen and full of dried blood.
His nose and cheek bones were fractured.
He looked like Rocky Balboa after one of his
boxing matches. He explained that he was
inside of a public bathroom adjacent to the
ship's casino. He stated that without reason
or warning, the perp walked in, grabbed him
and began to slam his head against the
urinal and steel plumbing pipes. He said the
man was visibly drunk and slammed his
face approximately 20 times. His parents
were enraged and wanted to see the man
prosecuted to the fullest extent of the law. I
obtained the ships coordinates, when the
incident occurred, and then contacted the

U.S. Coast Guard. They told me where the ship was at the time of the incident. It was in international waters, not far from Bermuda. I then called the Joint NYPD/FBI Task Force that investigates crimes that occur in international waters. The agent and detective I spoke with told me that the U.S. Attorney's Office refused to prosecute. I stood there at the dock, staring at the perp, the victim and his family. I'm supposed to stand there and let this perp walk free? Bullshit. I decided to arrest the guy anyway, and let the Manhattan District Attorney's Office tell me they couldn't come up with a charge to prosecute the perp on. In the meantime, I created a police report, obtained a written confession and obtained the perps pedigree information. Later, the District Attorney's Office declined to prosecute and I had to release the man. But I had created enough documentation and official paperwork for the victim and his family to at least sue the son of a bitch.

TAXIS

Types of Taxis.

As you leave the airport, bus, cruise ship or train terminal, one of your preferred modes of transportation is taxi. Unless you have previously arranged for private or commercial vehicle transportation, there are two types of taxis that you should look for. The two types of taxis are the traditional yellow taxi and the new light green taxis. The yellow taxis can pick you up and take you anywhere in the city. The green taxis can take you anywhere in the city, and pick you up anywhere in the city except at the airports and south of east 96th street and south of west 110th st. in Manhattan. The yellow and green taxis are licensed and inspected. At the minimum, each driver has gone through a background check and passed an examination. Their vehicles are also inspected, registered and maintained to meet government mechanical and emission standards.

Once you've entered your licensed and legal taxi, you should be relatively safe. If for some reason you don't feel safe, text a friend or family member. Give them the taxi number and/or the name of the driver. Both should be listed in the interior of the vehicle. As always though, go with your instinct. If you don't feel comfortable or safe, take another taxi. The overwhelming majority of taxi operators are hard working professionals. Many are immigrants from other countries and were professionals (doctors, lawyers, teachers, etc) in their respective countries. However, as with every profession, there are always a handful of bad apples.

Most likely, once you're in the taxi, you'll have a safe and uneventful journey. The majority of taxi related problems involve people who accidentally leave their cellphones, laptops, bags or other personal belongings when they exit the taxi at their destination. To prevent this from happening, leave your cellphone in your closed pocket or bag. If you take it out, simply be cognizant that you have it out and place it back in your pocket or bag. If any of your other items have straps, wrap the strap around your arm or leg. You won't forget them if they are attached to you. Above all, always remember that after you exit the taxi, pause, don't close the door.

Look back inside at the seat and the floor. Consciously think for a moment about what belongings you have or don't have with you.

When you reach your destination, you will have the option of paying by cash, cellphone app, credit or debit card. I suggest paying by credit or debit card. Why? Because if you do leave something behind you will have a record of the taxi you were in and may be able to track down your lost property. I would also suggest obtaining a receipt for the same reason. The agency that regulates NYC taxis is the Taxi & Limousine Commission. Should you have a complaint against a taxi driver or if you've lost your property inside an NYC taxi please call 311 and tell the operator your problem. The operator will connect your call or give you the appropriate telephone number to call.

One final safety tip pertaining to taxis. When you are exiting the vehicle, remember two things. First, only exit on the curbside of the street. Make sure that the door you are exiting from is adjacent to the sidewalk. Second, look before you exit. Many passengers get injured, injure passing bicyclists or cause vehicular accidents when they open taxi doors without looking. Save yourself the guilt, damage, lawsuit and injury to yourself or others and look first before you open the door.

Illegal Taxis.

For many decades, there has been a recurring problem with illegal or unlicensed taxis picking up passengers. These cars are not yellow or green and don't have meters. These drivers negotiate a price with you before you enter their car. Many tourists assume that this practice is normal and legal. Know that it is illegal. If you choose to enter one of these unlicensed vehicles, you may become a victim of kidnapping, sexual assault, robbery or overcharged. Additionally, the vehicle may not be properly maintained and mechanically unsafe.

Anecdote.

One of the first injuries I witnessed, while on duty, involved a taxi and a bicyclist. The taxi had pulled to the curb to discharge a passenger. The driver told the passenger to exit curbside because it was NYC law. The passenger ignored the driver's words and opened the door adjacent to the street. As he opened the door, a bicyclist was riding past. The door clipped the pedal of the bike and sent the cyclist flying into the air and into oncoming traffic. Two vehicles hit and ran over the cyclist. He survived but sustained numerous broken bones, cuts, scrapes and abrasions. The cyclist later sued the passenger for millions of dollars. Had the passenger simply opened the curbside door of the taxi, none of this would have happened.

HOTELS

Luggage Theft.

You've made it to the big city in one piece. You're now ready to arrive at your home away from home, your hotel. Your next task is getting your luggage and belongings safely into your room. There are individual and organized groups of thieves that patrol the exterior and interior of hotels searching for distracted travelers, unattended property and unlocked rooms. The primary way to not become a victim of one of these predators is to pay attention to your property. Do not leave your property unattended for even five seconds. Don't rely on stereotypes as well. These perpetrators are young, old, whites, blacks, hispanics, well dressed, poorly dressed, males, females, etc. I've seen perps dressed in suits and ties steal property as well as thieves in jeans and sneakers. Stealing is their full time job. The same way you have a job, this is theirs. They take it seriously and they study and practice their trade daily.

Don't leave your luggage curbside. You may think the bellhop or concierge are handling your items, but pause and look around. They are probably busy handling numerous other people and running in and out of the hotel. You can bicker with the hotel over who is responsible for your property after it's stolen, but at that point do you really care who's at fault? Or, would you just prefer that you had your property? Don't leave your items unattended.

Another group of thieves patrols the entrances of hotels. These thieves watch as people enter and exit hotel lobbies. They are pickpockets. As you enter the lobby revolving door, they will walk in with you. As the door revolves and you're wondering why they joined you in the door, they are skillfully stealing your wallet from your pocket or bag. As the door opens up into the lobby, you will exit, but they will remain in the door and exit back onto the street. You'll then see them flee using a waiting vehicle or on foot.

Interior Theft.

Once inside the hotel, you face another gauntlet of thieves. These thieves patrol hotel lobbies. They are looking for unattended baggage on the floor, bags hanging on the bellhop cart, etc. Again, keep an eye on your property and if you must leave items with the concierge, take your valuables with you.

You've made it to your hotel room, you're safe, right? Not quiet. While in your room, you are relatively safe. Close the door, engage the deadbolt and you should be fine. The threat in your hotel room occurs once you leave your room. There are individuals and organized groups that enter hotels daily and go floor to floor checking door handles. They are looking for doors that are unlocked, open or ajar. Upon exiting your room, check your door by pulling on the handle, to make sure it's locked. Take your valuables with you or leave them locked in your room safe. The safe can be defeated (rarely), but it's better to leave your valuables in the safe than not to. The true point of vulnerability is when housekeeping is cleaning your room. They tend to unlock and open more than one room at a time, thereby leaving at least one room unlocked, opened and unattended. This is an opportune time for one of these hallway creepers to enter your room without being noticed and steal your valuables if they are not stored in your safe. Once you return to your room and discover your property missing, housekeeping or other hotel employees may be wrongfully accused since they were the last people known to have entered your room. It should also be noted that it is not the norm, but some hotel staff have been caught stealing property from guests rooms.

If you're attending a business meeting in one of the hotel conference rooms keep an eye on your laptop. Most groups meet and when they break for lunch they leave their laptops in the conference room. The hotel creepers know this and patrol the conference rooms, waiting for groups to take their breaks. A well dressed creeper can enter a conference room, blend in as an attendee, pick up a laptop and simply walk away unnoticed. Don't leave your laptops unattended.

Prostitutes and Theft.

You've decided to go to the hotel bar or restaurant for some food or a drink. There are two types of criminal activity you should be aware of. The first involves unattended property. Even if you're in a group, keep an eye on your bags, pocketbook, etc. I have witnessed voluminous bag thefts from restaurants and bars. The most common victims were women who placed their bags on the floor or on the back of their chair. I've witnessed these crimes occur even when the victims were seated at a table with four or more people. The second type of criminal activity that commonly occurs in certain hotel bars and restaurants is prostitution. If you want to pick up a prostitute, you of course know it's illegal, but you should also know that most of these ladies of the night are also thieves. They prey on men that are intoxicated and that appear to have money or other valuables. They may walk with you to the atm, so you can obtain cash for payment. As you retrieve money they will look at and remember your pin number as you type it in. Later, in your room, when you are asleep, distracted or leave them alone while you're in the bathroom, they will steal your credit or debit card. They will then leave the room and head to the nearest atm, to withdraw as much money as possible. Another one of their methods is to approach you and talk to you. They will then begin to caress you all over your body. You think you're hot stuff and are enjoying an attractive woman fondling you and showing you some attention. Little do you know that she's stealing your valuables and/or your wallet. You should be alerted to this act when they abruptly stop fondling you and leave. They want to get away from you quickly, before you realize they have your property. Any one of these types of thefts can lead to not just emptying your bank and credit accounts, but also numerous fraudulent purchases and identity theft. Another method of thievery is the use of skimming devices. There has been a decline in the use of these devices, but they are still being used. A skimmer is a small electronic device that a server or bartender can fit in their pocket or apron. When you give them your credit or debit card to pay your bill, they walk away with your card and swipe it on their skimming device. This takes literally two seconds to do. Once swiped, all of your personal information attached to that account has been stored in that skimmer. They can then later reproduce an exact duplicate of your credit or debit card. Keep an eye on your cards and stay away from the hookers, you're not that hot.

The nexus between most, if not all, of these hotel thieves is that they are not looking to engage you. They are seeking property that is unattended or not being watched. They want to distract you while one of their colleagues steals your property without being detected. If you spot one of them in the act of stealing your property, most will drop the property and run, or take the property and run. They do not want to fight you for your property. In New York City it's a felony charge (severe) if you forcibly steal property from someone. It's a misdemeanor charge (light) if you steal unattended property valued at under one thousand dollars. A felony robbery charge could result in several years in jail. A misdemeanor petit larceny charge could result in just receiving a summons to appear in court at a later date. Generally, these perps don't want to fight you. They do not want to be caught and spend years in jail. Don't leave your property unattended.

If you become a victim of a crime while in a hotel, contact hotel security. They should contact the police. If they don't, then contact the police yourself (dial 911). The NYPD will work with hotel security and investigate the crime.

Anecdote.

I have hundreds of hotel crime related
stories. One stands out that involved a
degree of ignorance and racism. I was
serving in a plainclothes anti-crime unit. We
were responsible for locating criminals
before they committed crimes, following
them undetected, observing them
committing crimes and apprehending them.
We were a very proactive unit. I was in the
heart of Times Square, scanning the crowd
of tens of thousands. I picked up on a man
who I knew was going to pick someone's
pocket or bag. I profiled people on a daily
basis. Yes, I profiled people! But I based my
profiling on behavioral patterns, not race.
This particular perp was a thirty five year
old, white male, wearing a sharp business
suit. He stood out to me because of his
behavior. I saw him walking noticeably
slower than most of the other pedestrians. I
continued to blend into the throngs of
people and observe him. I then noticed that
he was staring at women who were carrying
pocketbooks. I continued to watch him as he
watched an asian woman carrying a
pocketbook. He followed her into the
revolving door of a busy and popular hotel.

I watched as they revolved in the door and he reached into her pocketbook and removed her purse. She exited into the hotel lobby and he continued, exiting back onto the street. She immediately noticed her purse was missing and ran outside. I had already apprehended the perp and had him in handcuffs when she approached me. This type of arrest was a typical one for me. What stood out was the statement the victim gave me. She said that she was visiting New York City for the first time and was from Japan. She stated, "I thought only black people stole." She stated that every movie she had seen in Japan showed black people as being bad. As a multi-racial 'cop', I spent the next hour interviewing her and giving her a real world lesson in crime, criminals and criminal behavior.

ATM'S

PIN and Card Theft.

You will need to obtain cash during your stay. You will most likely visit an atm more than one time during your stay. There are three criminal concerns that you should be aware of when visiting an atm. The first is the theft of your pin number. One method of obtaining your pin number is through direct observation. A criminal will pose as an atm customer and stand near enough to you where he or she can actually observe the numbers that you input into the keypad. The second method is a bit more technical. The criminals will actually place a hidden camera in the atm area. The camera is pointed at the keypad and will record the numbers you input onto the keypad. In conjunction with both of these methods, they will place a card reader on top of the bank's card reader. When you insert your card into the reader, your card information is stored in their card reader. Now the perps have enough of your information to clone an exact copy of your credit or debit card.

To prevent your pin number from being stolen, simply cover the keypad with your free hand as you input your pin number. This will prevent anyone next to you or a perps camera from observing the digits you are inputting. To prevent your card from being cloned, look at the card reader before you use it. Give it a tug or pull. If it's loose or doesn't appear normal, don't use it.

Theft and Robbery.

The last two concerns are theft and robbery. Some perps patrol atm areas and are looking for cash. The less sophisticated perps will simply walk into the atm area and watch as your money is dispensed from the machine. Once you have the money they will confront you. They will either demand that you give them your money (with or without a weapon) or they will actually physically attack you and take the money from you. The more sophisticated criminal(s) realize that the atm areas are full of cameras. These perps will observe you from outside of the atm area, purposely evading the bank cameras. They will watch as you receive your money and where you place it. They will then approach you several blocks away from the bank and demand the money or physically attack you and take the money from you (they watched where you placed it and know where its at).

The only way to prevent from becoming a victim of either of these two types of theft is awareness. You must be aware of who is around you. If you're in the atm area and someone else walks in and you feel uncomfortable, end your transaction without receiving money and walk out. If you obtained money and are exiting the atm area, walk a few paces and then look around. Observe who's around you and go with your instincts. They are usually correct.

Anecdote.

ATM related crime is abundant. My last atm related case involved an elderly woman who reported that her checking account had been wiped out through the use of her debit card. However, she possessed her debit card. After a few weeks of investigating, I determined that the woman had used her debit card at an atm machine located inside of a small deli. Perps had placed a card reader on top of the atm card reader. They stole her debit card information and produced a clone debit card. They then went on a shopping spree and purchased thousands of dollars worth of sneakers and furniture. Thankfully, these perps were the brightest bunch in the barrel. They had the merchandise delivered to their home, where we later apprehended them.

SUBWAYS

The NYC mass transit system is the best in the world, with subways and buses operating 365 days per year and 24 hours per day. With such 24/7 access in a city with more than 8 million residents and more than 52 million tourists per year, there are bound to be a multitude of crime related problems.

Electronic Device Theft.

A relatively new but persistent crime on the rails has been the theft of mobile devices (cellphones, laptops, tablets, etc). These perpetrators will snatch the devices directly out of your hands. One favorite technique is for the perp to stand inside the train or on the platform, adjacent to a subway car door. They watch as you stand or sit inside of the car and are focused on your device. As the door begins to close, the perp will snatch the device from your grasp and flee. The car door then closes and you get to watch as the perp flees and your train heads to the next station. As with most crimes, simple awareness can prevent this from happening to you. Pay attention to who's around you and don't have your device in your hand. A perp is not going to snatch and grab your property while the car doors are closed. They want to escape. So be extra vigilant when the car doors are open.

Sex Crimes.

Another crime that has occurred in the subway system for many decades is a crime called sexual abuse. The unofficial NYPD term for these perps is "weenie whacker". This is when a man will stand too close to you and begin to rub his private parts against you or touch your private parts. He may do this by actually exposing his penis or leaving it in his pants. This occurs daily in the subway system. I've witnessed white, black, hispanic and asian, elderly and youthful offenders commit these acts. After talking to many of these perps, they commit these acts for several reasons. One is sexual gratification. The other is power. Lastly, they enjoy the thrill of getting away with doing this in public. The victims of this crime include the elderly, adult women and underage boys and girls. Some of the perps are obvious and their victims realize what is happening. Other perps are more subtle and conduct their acts during rush hour in crowded subway cars, making it more difficult to detect. There's only one way to possibly prevent this from occurring to you. Sit in a seat or stand with your back next to the door. You don't want anyone behind you. These perps are generally committing this act while standing behind you. If you are a victim of this crime, alert the train conductor or the police. If there are no police officers present, the conductor will request a police response via two way radio.

In conjunction with the sexual abuse crimes are the 'upskirt' perps. These perps covertly take pictures under women's skirts with their cell phones. They tend to commit their acts while walking behind women on staircases or in crowded trains where their actions can be easily concealed. This act is a crime. Alert a police officer or Transit worker if you feel you have been a victim of this crime.

Pickpockets.

Pickpockets love crowds. It's easier to pick someones pocket or bag while in a crowd. The subway system is a crowded place where being bumped is typical. Pickpockets may use those typical bumps and crowds to disguise their actions. A solid bump against your arm will distract you from any movement that may have occurred in your pocket or bag as they steal your wallet or purse. To prevent from being a victim of one of these perps, I suggest carrying your wallet in your front pant pocket. It's extremely difficult to steal a wallet from a snug fitting front pant pocket. If you are carrying a shoulder bag. Carry the main portion of the bag in front of you, not on your side or behind you. These perps don't want you to know they are taking your property and they don't want to get caught. If the main portion of your bag is in front of you, then they will be unable to take anything without you noticing.

Minor Crimes.

Numerous minor crimes occur daily in the subway system. Most of them you shouldn't worry about. These other crimes include people standing by subway entrances offering to swipe their metro card for you, allowing you entry into the system, for a discounted price. Don't buy swipes or metro cards from people. It's illegal. You may encounter homeless people and performers on the trains and on the platforms. They are seeking donations. You can give them money if you want, but understand that potential perps may be watching you as you pull out your wallet and money. You could be setting yourself up to be a crime victim.

Serious Crime.

Serious and violent crimes also occur in the subway system. If someone is going to approach you and stab or rob you, there's not much you can do to prevent this from happening, other than to be aware of your surroundings. I would suggest riding in the center car, where the conductor is located. I would also suggest riding in the first car, where the train motorman (operator) operates he train. I would not suggest riding in the last car. The last cars of subway trains are notorious for being preferred locations for criminal activity.

Emotionally Disturbed People (EDP).

The biggest problem in the subway system is people. It's a crowded and enclosed environment with people from across the globe. Each person has their own varying level of emotional competence or incompetence. Riding amongst the emotionally stable people however are emotionally disturbed people. This is a politically correct term for crazy people. Verbal and physical altercations between passengers is a semi-normal occurrence, especially during rush hour. If someone engages you in what you think could become a verbal or physical altercation. I suggest walking away or downplaying the conversation. Stay in populated areas though. Don't walk to desolate areas where there are less people.

Every year, people are pushed onto subway tracks and injured or killed by oncoming trains. You never know who the person next to you is nor do you know their emotional state. My suggestion here is to simply stand away from the edge of the subway platform and with your back against the wall. Once the train enters the station and comes to a complete stop, then proceed to walk over to board it. Standing at the edge of the platform is just not smart and unnecessary.

Anecdote.

While traveling with lights and sirens blaring in our unmarked police car, my partner and I were flagged down by a man standing in the street. We could not understand what he was saying, but he was directing us to the adjacent subway entrance. We jumped out of our car and headed down into the subway system. As we approached the platform level, we observed six people attempting to hold a man. Our cheap suits were no disguise. They knew we were detectives. They immediately told us that the man had been taking pictures of another man's wife with a cellphone. They stated that they were on a train and observed the man with his cell phone under the woman's dress. The woman's husband, a police detective from Austria, was holding the man's phone and showed me one photo that the perp had taken. The perp confessed to the crime and we hauled his ass to jail.

STREET SAFETY

You've made it out of your hotel room and you're ready to explore the big city. Crime is down overall by about 80%, citywide, since 1992. However, you're still in a big city, so your safety and survival rests in your hands and your ability to stay aware of your surroundings. There are many hazards on the streets of New York City.

Vehicles.

One of your biggest hazards are vehicles, bicyclists and pedicabs. Every year, tens of thousands of people in NYC are struck by these modes of transportation. Pedestrians have the right of way when walking in streets, but remember something that I always tell people. Think of your grade school days, sitting in science class. What's stronger? Metal or muscle and bone? I say metal wins every time. Yes, you can keep walking in front of that car because legally you have the right of way. But, encounter a distracted driver or an angry driver (there are many), then you might find yourself in the hospital or a casket. It's not worth it. You have the right of way, but use that right with caution. That law does you no good if you're dead. You also have to be aware of the voluminous number of vehicles that crash, lose control and end up hitting pedestrians on the sidewalk. You don't want to be paranoid about looking for cars. However, I suggest just making it a point to turn your head and look whenever you hear a tire screech or crashing sounds.

Sidewalks and Streets.

Some of the hazards you'll encounter on the sidewalks and streets are open basements, cracks, uneven pavement and holes. One of the less obvious dangers are the metal covers that are embedded in the city streets and sidewalks. Beneath these metal covers are the city sewer system, steam network, cable television and electrical systems. There are thousands of these covers in the city. Several times per year, some of these explode. You do not want to be standing on top of one of these when they blow up. The typical causes are corrosion or over heating. Once corroded, the electrical system covers can become conduits for electricity. People and the dogs that they have been walking have received electrical shocks from walking on these corroded electrical system covers.

The biggest safety concern while walking the streets of NYC are vehicles and cyclists. You must truly understand that you aren't in Kansas anymore when walking the streets of NYC. Before you step off the sidewalk and into the street, look both ways for vehicles and cyclists. The bike lanes are a particular new hazard. People are not use to looking out for cyclists barreling down the dedicated bicycle lanes at high rates of speed. The cyclists are also not expecting pedestrians to step off the sidewalk and into their path without looking first. Vehicles present the same hazard. There are literally hundreds of vehicular accidents each day in NYC. Most are minor, but some are serious. You must walk these streets coherent of these hazards.

Pickpockets.

When walking, carry your strap bag on the front of your body or the side of your body. Carry it on the back of your body and you are at risk of being a target for one of the many individual or organized pickpocketing groups that patrol NYC. The favorite target of these perps are woman, walking with their bags hanging off of their shoulders and against their backs. For the men, I suggest carrying your wallet in your front pant pocket and not your rear pant pocket. The rear pocket is a favorite for pickpockets who are trained experts at taking your wallet without you noticing. When dealing with pickpockets, the term, "safety in numbers", does not apply. I have witnessed professional organized groups pick pockets and bags, undetected amongst large groups of people.

Another preferred method that pickpockets use is the distraction method. This method requires at least two perps. One perp engages you in conversation. He/she might be posing as a lost tourist or may physically bump into you. The purpose of this interaction is to distract you as his/her partner steals your property. Other methods include one perp taking a ketchup or other small condiment package and spilling it on your back. He/she then approaches you and offers to help clean it off of you. While you are engaged and dealing with that mess, the other perp is focused on stealing your property undetected. Another method involves one of the perps throwing money down in front of you. As you bend down to pick it up, the other perp is focused on stealing your property.

Scams.

There are too many scams for me to print them all here. Your best defense against these scams is to remember the old saying, "If it's too good to be true, it's probably not true." If a guy approaches you and offers to sell you a Rolex watch for $500. Don't negotiate him down to $300 and think that you got a great deal on a Rolex. What you purchased was a counterfeit $3 watch that will break within a day of purchasing it. If someone offers to sell you an in the box, brand new 32 inch television for $50. Know that when you get to your hotel room and open up that box, you'll most likely have a box that contains rocks, bricks or a broken 32 inch television. If you're looking for fake identification, drugs or prostitutes and you give someone money to get the product or prostitute for you, know that you will probably never see that person or your money again. Don't let your own greed or the offer of such a good deal make you forget good 'ole common sense.

Serious Crimes.

Serious and violent crime are down in NYC.
Once again though, you are in the largest
city in the nation. Big city crime does
happen in the big city. Terrorism, murder,
rape, armed robbery, shootings and
stabbings still occur in NYC. Their
frequency though is extremely low, so I
would not be overly concerned. If you
maintain your normal awareness, listen to
your gut instinct, and react appropriately,
you should be fine.

Anecdote.

One of my first scam related arrests
involved a group of four 19 year old boys
from New Jersey. They came to the precinct
and reported that they were robbed at
gunpoint. It took me about 5 seconds to
realize that they were in town to purchase
fake identification cards. However, none of
them admitted this. They stated that as
they were exploring the city, a man
approached them, pulled out a gun and
demanded their money. After about 30

minutes of interviewing them, they confessed to what really happened. They came to NYC to purchase fake identification cards. They conversed with a man on the street who said he could get them fake NYS drivers licenses. They gave him $400 for the licenses. The perp told them to wait for him inside of a deli while he went to retrieve the licenses. The boys waited an hour. He never returned. There was no gun involved nor any threat or robbery. They were simply scammed while the were trying to obtain illegal and counterfeit government identification. For wasting my time, I arrested each of them for filing a false police report.

RESTAURANTS, BARS AND CLUBS

You're looking for some good food, a drink or a night out dancing. You'll most likely have an uneventful good time, but there are some things you should be aware of. The following applies to five star locations equally as one star locations.

Bag Theft.

Once again, the name of the game is awareness. Pay attention to your property. On a daily basis, I observe people walk away from their bags or cell phones, to go use the bathroom or hit the dance floor. And on a daily basis I've observed perpetrators steal this property. Detectives are then tasked with spending countless numbers of hours investigating these thefts and the subsequent fraudulent credit card purchases and identity theft. You are ultimately responsible for your own property, not a facility or the police.

As I've previously discussed, bags being stolen from the backs of chairs is an extremely common occurrence. Never leave your bag hanging from the back of your chair, even if you're sitting in it, and even if you're seated next to other people. A professional thief will target you and take your bag without you or them noticing.

Roofies.

A more vile crime, that occurs frequently, deals with leaving your drink unattended. Bartenders, patrons and others have been known to "roofie" drinks. The term roofie is slang for a narcotic that is usually colorless, tasteless and odorless that can incapacitate you by making you unconscious or semiconscious. The person usually slips the roofie into your drink while you're not paying attention to your drink. Once you consume a drink that has been tainted, you can expect within minutes to feel like a freight train just hit you. You must try to stay with your trusted friends or family or attempt to make it to a very public area and announce what happened. I would also suggest calling 911 and explaining what happened and exactly where you are. Time is of the essence because you will be unconscious, or semiconscious, and incapacitated within minutes. Overall, you'll want to seek immediate medical attention. The medical facility will assist you and take samples to determine if you have consumed a roofie. They will be able to save the samples as evidence to assist the police with investigating the incident and prosecuting whomever committed this crime. There are usually one of two reasons why someone will roofie a person. The usual reason is a male wants to have sex with a girl. He will roofie her in an attempt to take advantage of her once the drug takes effect. This also occurs in the gay community, with a male committing the act against another male. Men and women will roofie guys to steal their wallets and other valuable property once the male victim is incapacitated.

Violent Crime.

In general, you must be careful of your surroundings and who and what is going on around you. I've witnessed one too many shootings, stabbings and fights because two people bumped into each other or someone was staring at someone's significant other for too long. I suggest that if an altercation starts, simply walk away. To get stabbed, shot or engaged in a fight over something as stupid as accidentally bumping someone, or staring at someone's girl, is beyond stupid. Too many thousands of people have lost their lives or been maimed for one of these stupid reasons.

Anecdote.

This one wasn't a crime I investigated. This occurred to a close personal friend of mine. She was in a nightclub to meet two male friends. Everything was fine, but she did recall that she had left her drink unattended a few times. She stated that all of a sudden, like a punch in her face, she felt heavy and weak. The room was spinning and she felt her legs getting weak and her vision began to fail. She described how she stumbled to a bench, where several guys were drinking bottles of vodka. She wanted to ask them to help her, but she could not get the words out. Not realizing her true condition, the men began pouring vodka down her throat, laughing and dancing. She said that she used her last ounce of energy, fell to the floor and rolled under the bench where she felt she would be safe. She was one of the lucky ones. Bouncers later saw her and called 911 for an ambulance to respond. She was taken to the hospital, where she was treated and tested. She had been drugged/roofied. Surveillance footage

in the club was poor and no one was charged
with this crime. She was indeed though one
of the lucky ones.

LAWS YOU SHOULD KNOW

We all know about laws such as murder, rape, robbery and burglary. These and other crimes are what I call common sense crimes. They are acts we all know are illegal, regardless of what country or state you are from. What I'm going to describe in this section are laws that aren't as obvious. I won't focus on the actual names of each law. I will focus on what's important to know, the action that makes what you are doing illegal.

Alcohol.

You cannot walk on the streets with an open container of alcohol. That means you cannot walk down the street with a cup of alcohol (including beer) or an open bottle of wine or liquor. This also applies to motor vehicles. You cannot operate a motor vehicle with an open container of alcohol in it (even if you're a passenger).

DRIVING.

Yes, New York City does have a posted speed limit. The speed limit in NYC is 25 miles per hour, unless otherwise posted (*As of November, 2014). There are no right turns on a red light in NYC, unless otherwise posted. You're in NYC, not a third world country. All normal traffic laws apply (use your turn signal to change lanes, wear your seat belt, etc.).

Subways.

It is illegal to pass through the alarmed doors at the subway entrances (unless there's an emergency or permitted by a transit worker or police officer). It is illegal to lay across subway seats. It is illegal to smoke in the subway system. This includes open air or above ground platforms and entrance and exit staircases. It is illegal to enter subway tunnels or walk on subway tracks.

Streets.

It is still illegal to possess or smoke marihuana, even for medicinal purposes

(*As per Federal law). NYC law however makes possession of less than 25 grams of marihuana a ticket able offense. Though very rarely enforced, it is illegal to cross the street when the traffic light is not in your favor (green). It is illegal to urinate or defecate in public. If walking a dog, you must pick up and dispose of its fecal matter.

* The most important thing to know about these and other laws is that you can be arrested for violating any of these laws. A typical stay in a New York City jail can last one to three days before you see a judge.

EVENTS YOU SHOULD KNOW

West Indian Day Parade.

Every Labor Day (September), the West
Indian Day Parade kicks off at midnight, in
Brooklyn. There are a million participants
and spectators. It's a wonderful and festive
event, with the majority of people there to
celebrate and have fun. However, every
year, there are serious and violent crimes
that occur during this event. I worked the
event numerous times, and every year
there were multiple shootings, stabbings,
sexual assaults, assaults on police officers
and other crimes that occurred.

St. Patrick's Day Parade.

This is a wonderful event that occurs each
year on St. Patrick's Day. Most participants
and spectators attend to have fun and enjoy
the sights. But the day is also notorious for

underage drinking, fights and disorderly conduct.

National Puerto Rican Day Parade.

Every May or June NYC hosts the National Puerto Rican Day Parade. It's a very festive and fun event. Most folks in attendance are there to dance, sing, and watch the festivities. Every year though, there are a few hooligans and gang members that show up and create some problems. One notorious year, there were numerous sexual assaults on women.

Rockefeller Center Christmas Tree Lighting.

What criminal element could be out and about infecting this beautiful event? Weenie whackers and pickpockets. As you lean against the marble wall to look down at the skating rink, glance behind you from time to time. There are perverted bastards getting their jollies off by rubbing their exposed or concealed private parts against gawkers. These perps come in all races and ages and victimize the young and the old. The pickpockets also come in all ages, races and genders. The crowds are thicker than any on the planet. This is their heaven. It's easy pickin's as everyone is bumping into and touching each other. Regarding both of these crimes, you wouldn't recognize an intentional inappropriate bump from an accidental bump. Follow the advice I've offered throughout this book and you should be able to avoid these perps.

SUMMARY

New York City is a wonderful city. It's arguably the best city on the planet. You can spend a lifetime here and never see and do everything that this city has to offer. When you visit, you will most likely have a very safe and uneventful experience. Forget the low crime statistics, you will also actually feel safe during your visit. The NYPD is the largest police agency in the United States. There are more than 20 other law enforcement agencies that operate in New York City. NYC is safer than Orlando, Florida (One of my favorite places). Who would have ever imagined that fact? Old time New Yorkers who lived in NYC during its violent days have now nicknamed the city "DisneyLand". If you have any non emergency related questions about city services, call 311. If you have a police, medical or fire emergency, call 911.

Enjoy yourself during your stay, but maintain a degree of awareness. Don't let

the stats and true feeling of safety fool you.
There are still plenty of perps out here
looking for victims. Remember to not be
tricked by your personal stereotypes of
perps. They come in all shapes, sizes, races,
religions and ages. I've witnesed Hasidic
Jews commit crimes, as well as Christians,
Catholics, Muslims and others. I've
witnessed gorgeous runway models commit
crimes, as well as professional business
women. I've witnessed wealthy and affluent
men commit crimes, as well as popular
celebrities. Don't think you'll be able to spot
the majority of these criminals, you won't.
Don't forget the overwhelming majority of
crime that does exist in NYC is not violent
crime. Property and financial crime are the
crimes of the day in modern NYC. Your
chance of becoming a crime victim is very
small. If you are the victim of a crime, it will
most likely be related to some type of theft
or other non-violent crime.

As you explore the city, note how often and
frequent you see a police presence. Compare
your observations to the police presence in
the city or country where you are from. You
are probably safer in NYC than you are in
your hometown. If you follow my advice, I
guarantee you that you will have a virtually

crime and incident free experience during your stay. You might also find some of my advice useful and applicable in your own hometown.

From a man who has devoted his life to helping others, thank you for allowing me to share my insight with you.

- Mike Greene -

17204236R00045

Made in the USA
Middletown, DE
11 January 2015